30 Days
TO A
Better You

30 Days TO A *Better You*

A GUIDE TO PEACE, LIBERATION, AND SELF-REFLECTION

SHIRLEY WALKER-KING

30 DAYS TO A BETTER YOU
Published by Purposely Created Publishing Group™
Copyright © 2020 Shirley Walker-King
All rights reserved.

No part of this book may be reproduced, distributed or transmitted in any form by any means, graphic, electronic, or mechanical, including photocopy, recording, taping, or by any information storage or retrieval system, without permission in writing from the publisher, except in the case of reprints in the context of reviews, quotes, or references.

Scriptures marked NIV are taken from the New International Version®. Copyright © 1973, 1978, 1984, 2011 by Biblica, Inc.™. All rights reserved.

Printed in the United States of America

ISBN: 978-1-64484-138-9

Special discounts are available on bulk quantity purchases by book clubs, associations and special interest groups.
For details email: sales@publishyourgift.com
or call (888) 949-6228.
For information log on to www.PublishYourGift.com

Dedicated to the women in my family who have gained their wings of glory and are now angels. Thank you for your love, sacrifices, and strength. Because of you, I will carry the torch and not be afraid to live, laugh, and love.

"For he will command his angels concerning you to guard you in all your ways."
—Psalm 91:11 (NIV)

To my:
Great-Grandmother
Elwilder Wilson Jackson of Opelousas, LA

Grandmother
Ruby Lee Jackson Shelton of Cheek, TX

Great Aunts
Shirley Marie Jackson, Estia Mae Jackson, Freda "Nanny" Davis, and Bessie Mae Lewis

Aunt
Joyce Maria Herman McBride of Beaumont, TX

Cousins
Dolores Justice and Makayla Faith Ann Davis, Edna "Renee" Knight, and Linda F. Coleman

TABLE OF CONTENTS

Acknowledgments ix
Foreword xi
Introduction 1

Day 1: Learn to Love Yourself 7
Day 2: Believe in Yourself 10
Day 3: Savor the Moment 13
Day 4: Make You a Priority 16
Day 5: Learn Something New 20
Day 6: Mix It Up, Make New Friends, or Find
  a Mentor 23
Day 7: Stretch Your Mind, Body, and Soul 26
Day 8: Start Living to Your Full Potential 30
Day 9: Create a Routine and Track Your Progress 33
Day 10: Think Positively 35
Day 11: Hold Yourself Accountable 38
Day 12: Start Looking for the Silver Lining 40
Day 13: Start Enjoying the Things You Already
  Have 43
Day 14: Open Your Heart 45
Day 15: Nurture Your Current Relationships 48
Day 16: Stop a Bad Habit 51
Day 17: Concentrate on What You Can Control 53

Day 18: Forgiving Yourself 55
Day 19: Cheer for Other People 59
Day 20: Be Yourself 62
Day 21: Listen to Yourself 65
Day 22: Push Past Your Comfort Zone 68
Day 23: Say Thank You 71
Day 24: Spend Time in Nature 74
Day 25: Volunteer to Help the Less Fortunate 78
Day 26: Write a Gratitude Journal 82
Day 27: Living Each Day with Purpose 85
Day 28: Let Go of the Anger 88
Day 29: Understand Your Strengths 91
Day 30: Connect with Something Higher
   Than You 96

Testimonies 101
About the Author 105

ACKNOWLEDGMENTS

I am forever grateful to my mother, Shirley Ann Locke Johnson, my mother-in-law, Jacqueline D. Wright, and my sister, Tracey Walker Pollard. Thank you for believing in me and allowing me to use you as my test tube ladies! You ladies inspire and encourage me to live beyond limits.

I carry your voice with me everywhere I go, never stopping and never accepting no.

To my husband, Vincent King, I love you, respect you, and trust you with my soul.

You are the reason I smile from the inside out.
Your love for me I will never doubt.
You've loved me in good times and bad.
When I've been happy and when I've been sad.
You trusted me and never gave up.
Keeping your promise "we are in this 'together' until the end"
And for that, I will always love you as my lover, my husband, and my friend.

To my daughter, Valencia King, words cannot express the joy you bring.

You are the reason I breathe, my heart, my everything.

Your father holds the key to my soul.

Giving birth to you made me whole.

I thank God for you every day and pray He leads you the right way.

I will always be here for you as a mother, a sister, and yes, a friend.

Thank you for paying attention to the words I said and giving them back to me when needed.

FOREWORD

What is your purpose? What do you want out of life? What's your heart's desire? You can have it all and more if you focus on making a better you. It is an energy that only you can produce when designing your life to create a better version of yourself, and now, you have taken the first step in your new plan of action.

I have had the privilege of knowing Mrs. SWK, Shirley Walker-King, as we know her! Shirley assists in keeping my foundation, Kier's Hope, running smoothly. She is a remarkable person who is dependable and strives to get things done efficiently and effectively.

Reading this book is a great way to start becoming a better you. May you gain direction for your life from this book and from God who is always in control and making everything possible.

As a son, comedian, writer, entrepreneur, and advocate for sickle cell, every day I take with me the fundamentals, will, and know-how of making a better me. May this book and the next thirty days be a "jump start" to a better you!

Shirley has given you a great guide and outline to do that, and now, you can apply this to your everyday life. Go forth and start! A better you is a thought that starts in your head and now you are taking steps to make it a reality. Remember you don't have to wait until New Years to get a NEW BETTER YOU together; there is always tomorrow. Success starts for you today. You have the first step. Read it.

> *"The Light of Greatness shines upon me,*
> *and because I showed up, the world*
> *will never be the same."*
>
> —Les Brown

Kier "Junior" Spates
Alicia's son
Granny's favorite
Child of God
Emmy-nominated writer
Radio personality
Entrepreneur
Comedian
Actor

INTRODUCTION

I am honored to share this journey with you. Your being here says to me you, too, feel the way I sometimes feel—like there is something more than this. Your something or your "this" may look and feel different than my something or my this, but the feeling is the same. Your this may be related to health, relationships, fitness, family, finances, or even spiritual. All of these factors can take a toll on your overall well-being. Throughout life, we will all go through ups and downs, trials, and tribulations, which can distract us from becoming the best version of ourselves. We give, give, and give until we have nothing left of ourselves to give. It's time to seize the day and take back control and work on being a better you for your future.

It goes without saying we are all on a journey to be the best person we can be. We all want happiness, love, success, and prosperity, right? Most of us believe if we can just do things faster and better than the next person, it will improve our lives and get us one step closer to our goal of being perfect. Well, that old saying "practice makes perfect" is slightly misleading. The hardcore truth is, no one is perfect and no one will ever be perfect. The truth of the matter is practice simply makes you better than you were before. But please don't give up on yourself just keep practicing being the best person you can be. We are all on a journey to become the best person we want to be – right? It's very important to take time to re-energize, re-evaluate, and take inventory of your life. There's no time like the present. Right now is the best time for you to stop and smell the roses.

As a wife, mother, daughter, sister, friend, and community leader, I get overwhelmed with the day to day hustle and bustle of life. I lead a very active life, playing professional and recreational basketball, doing aerobics, dancing, and even kickboxing until life sets in and hits me from the left and the right with situation after situation. I spent two years dealing with various levels of depression. Yes, I said the "D" word, not divorce but depression. Oh, you don't think there are levels of depression? Well, there are. Depression can be mild, moderate, major, or even chronic. Depression can be triggered by stressful life changes from the death of a love one, divorce, a move, job loss, financial challenges, social isolation, medical and mood disorders, or even as a result of exposure to certain medications. Many people deal with and suffer from depression in silence, and they don't have to. Depression occurs more often than we think, and it occurs more often in women than in men. Depression shows up in various ways from feeling low, sad, and lonely at times to persistently feeling left out, worthless, and even guilty. After almost eight months of healing from an Achilles injury at the age of 43, I thought I could survive anything. However, having to go through surgery and depend on others to help me on a daily basis took a physical toll on me but not even that could prepare me for the aftermath of an unpredictable auto accident that left hardly any external injuries but left a lasting internal dilemma and post-traumatic stress disorder (PTSD). On top of dealing with the short and long-term effects of the auto accident, I lost clients, and I had to return to corporate America working a 9 to 5 job, forgetting about my entrepreneurial goals. I had to deflect the societal pressures of being a superwoman and dealing with aging parents. My mother had a stroke, and my mother in-law had blood clots. My marriage was being attacked, and people I called friends betrayed me. All of these things kept me from being the Shirley I knew, loved, and desired to be. It was at that moment I realized I had lost myself, and my life was out of balance. With the help of my husband, Vincent, daughter, Valencia, and primary care physician and therapist, whose name is also Shirley, I slowly regained the courage to look in the mirror and take back control of my well-being and myself.

It took time for me to redefine who I am and get back to being the best version of myself. I had to reflect on what was holding me back from operating to my fullest potential. So, I did, and I want to help guide you on the very journey I took to becoming a better me one day at a time. I literally told immediate family and friends I was not checking out on them, but I was checking in on Shirley, and for the next 30 days, I was solely working on me!

For the next 30 days, I want to share with you and show you how focusing on you will change the way you feel, think, and respond to the hustle and bustle called life. I am not saying the next 30 days will change your life in every area, but it will jumpstart your journey to becoming the best version of you, and that starts with putting you first. I encourage you to truly think about your needs. Stop putting yourself last and stop feeling sorry for yourself. I did! Instead of feeling sorry for myself, I had to pull it together, get counseling, and get back to self-validation. I encourage you to seek guidance from a trained professional. Whether that's your primary care physician, therapist, counselor, or spiritual adviser, I encourage you to invite them into your world with the intention of becoming a better you.

When you declare your intention of becoming the best you, you tell the universe and those around you:

- Who you want to be.
- How you plan to be that person.
- How you choose to live your life with a purpose.

Your intentions of becoming the best you will touch and make a difference in the lives of others; just wait and see. Let's start the journey.

I have always been a journaling person. I have poems, lyrics to songs, and books written on pieces of paper all around my house and office. Things come to me, and I write them down, knowing it will connect with something sooner or later. To keep you from scattering your journals like me, I am adding an area after each day for you to journal about your experience. This will help you be in the moment, stay in the moment, and repeat the moment as needed. Studies show journaling helps prioritize your thoughts and track your progress, and it's a healthy way to express yourself. For me, journaling helped me control my depression and deal with my premenopausal mood swings. Writing in a journal as we go through the next 30 days will help you create order. It will help you truly be a better person as you reflect on who you want that person to be. I suggest you pick a place that is relaxing and accessible, maybe even grab a cup of tea. Ready? Let's start the journey of discovering things to do that will make you better day by day, so you don't look back one day and wish you had made a change, and done things differently or better. When we see people at their best, it inspires us to want to do better and be our best. So, I encourage you to be that person others see and say, "If she/he can do it, I can do it too!"

Extra-Extra Read All About It!
Because I am a spiritual being and a woman full of words of encouragement, I will share quotes from the Bible, poems, and inspirational quotes. I believe the Bible is our guide, our employee handbook for all things in life. And well, poems and quotes are gathered thoughts and responses to this unpredictable life we live.

    Let's get started!

Day 1

Learn to Love Yourself

"Therefore, as God's chosen people, holy and dearly loved, clothe yourselves with compassion, kindness, humility, gentleness and patience."

–Colossians 3:12, NIV

Learning to love yourself starts with making a conscious decision to be JOYFUL. Notice I said joyful and not happy. To me being joyful is different than being happy. Happy is a feeling, an emotion that depends on circumstances. Joyful is a gift from God, a divine internal truth. Joyful can't be given or taken away, so no one can control your joy.

How you see yourself shapes your reality. Remember, no one cares more about you and your future than you. Only you can ensure you stay on the right path of self-love and self-respect. This has to be a daily affirmation: "I love me some me." Every day won't be a win where you break out the champagne, but as long as you can say you did your best and loved yourself while you did it, it's a huge start.

"I Love Me."

Journal:

_____

_____

_____

_____

_____

_____

_____

_____

_____

_____

30 Days to a Better You

Day 2

Believe in Yourself

"Optimism is the faith that leads to achievement. Nothing can be done without hope and confidence."

–Helen Keller

Whatever it is that you want to do, get done, accomplish, or achieve stop waiting for someone else to pick you. Instead pick yourself and get started. If you want to make more money, stop waiting on your boss or company to raise your salary. Instead, turn your hobby into an additional source of income in your spare time. Believe in yourself because you are who God says you are. Say this out loud: "I am who I am, and I am proud to be ME. I am significant because (fill in the blank)."

_____

_____

_____

_____

_____

And here are three ways my significance impacts my life and the life of others:

1. _____
   _____

2. _____
   _____

3. _____
   _____

Journal:

_____
_____
_____
_____
_____
_____
_____
_____

Shirley Walker-King

Day 3

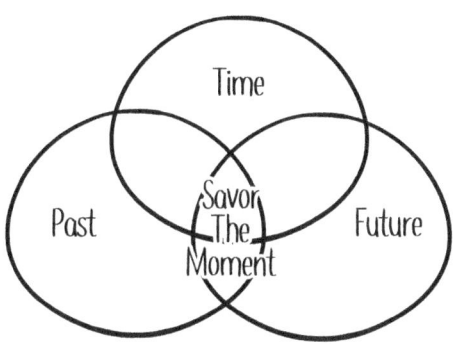

Savor the Moment

"You can't live in the past, and you can't predict the future. What you have to do right now, my child, is enjoy this very moment."

–Shirley Ann Locke Johnson (my mother)

My mother told me that around the age of sixteen I was so busy trying to figure out what I really wanted to do: play basketball, run track, or model. I was so overwhelmed with options that I did not take a moment to realize I was fortunate enough to have options. She reminded me that not all people have options, talent, or a skill, and I needed to just relax and savor the moment. Her teaching me to savor the moment at a young age allowed me to focus on the opportunity not the outcome. Right now, I need you to focus on the opportunity. Savoring the moment forces you into the present, so you can't worry about things that aren't there. Start focusing on the possibilities, and positive outcomes will follow.

Journal:

30 Days to a Better You

Day 4

Make You a Priority

"Be who you are and say what you feel, because in the end those who mind don't matter, and those who matter don't mind."

–Dr. Seuss

Why do we always fail to prioritize ourselves? We often tend to put other people's needs before our own. We feel guilty for saying no and eventually catch that disease to please. It's a sickness that has a cure. The cure is called putting you first. The cure is to start genuinely and proudly making yourself your number one priority. You are your greatest asset, cheerleader, and resource - now act like it! It's time for you to take a good look in the mirror and take the first steps to making yourself a priority. Especially if you are a parent, you may be asking yourself how can this woman tell me to put myself first? That's unheard of and a difficult concept to grasp. But as my mother once told me, "You can't take care of nobody if you ain't here." Mind blowing, right?

Making yourself your priority does not mean you are going to be selfish; it means you are going to be self-aware. Here are three ways you can make yourself more of a priority:

1. Be your own cheerleader!

You have to stick up for yourself and realize your self-worth. Don't allow others to determine your time, your schedule, and your priority level. Focus on what you can control and remember your needs are important too! Know that you are enough.

2. Set boundaries and adjust your expectations of yourself and those around you.

Setting boundaries with the people in your life is the ultimate life changer. There is no shame in saying no. You can be kind yet firm without being rude. I find that people respect my directness, and when I offer an alternative, that is a bonus. Treat yourself with respect and others will follow.

3. Learn to delegate.

I know most of us are used to rolling up our sleeves and getting the job done. Well, learning to delegate keeps your sleeves wrinkle-free and gives someone else an opportunity to grow. Once I learned to let go, I felt like more of a leader and mentor than I ever had. Letting go and delegating freed my time to teach others new skills as well as taught me to trust others capabilities.

Journal:

What can you delegate today that will give you time to focus on a high-level task?

What can you delegate, let go of, or release tomorrow that will allow someone else the opportunity to learn, grow, develop a new skill, or just plain figure it out? *I say just figure it out because sometimes people just have to figure it out on their own...*

Day 5

Learn Something New

"Anyone who stops learning is old, whether at twenty or eight."

–Henry Ford

I don't know about you, but I have always been curious about my surroundings and the world. I've always had this thing for learning something new. I have a degree in human relations and business and over eight certifications. Those who know me know I pride myself on being a jack of all trades and a master of many. It's my own sense of accomplishment and pride. There are many benefits to learning new things such as:

- You make connections between skills. Remember that old saying, "the more you know the more you grow?" It's true.
- You become a more interesting person.
- It changes your perception about things around you and makes it easy to adapt to change.

Expand your knowledge by honing in on your skills through reading, attending seminars, taking classes, and surrounding yourself with like-minded professionals.

Journal:

What new skill, adventure, or idea do you want to explore?

_____
_____
_____
_____
_____
_____
_____
_____
_____
_____
_____
_____

Shirley Walker-King

Day 6

Mix it up, Make New Friends, or Find a Mentor

"Surround yourself only with people who are going to take you higher."

–Oprah Winfrey

Start spending time with the right people; surround yourself with other positive and productive people with similar interests. Start giving new people you meet a chance; be ready to meet someone who might just change your situation, or you might be the person to change their situation.

Places to meet new people:
- Book clubs
- While traveling
- Work environment
- At the gym
- Volunteering
- At church

- Festival
- Trying something new

If you chose to find a mentor:

a. Identify the type of person you would like to mentor you and ask (relentless and respectfully).
b. Be willing to learn, grow, and be challenged.
c. Be willing to give and invest in the relationship and stay committed to the process.
d. Pay it forward - Help others beyond what your mentor has helped you accomplish.

Journal:

_____
_____
_____
_____
_____
_____
_____
_____

30 Days to a Better You

Day 7

Stretch Your Mind, Body, and Soul

"Nothing will work unless you do."

—Maya Angelou

According to science, we use less than 10 percent of our brains. We confine ourselves to past experiences. Studies suggest as we get older, we lose our curiosity and have conditioned ourselves not to stretch our minds without even realizing it. Starting today, take 10 minutes to relax and stretch your mind, body, and soul.

1. Let your mind explore the possibilities.

2. Stretch your body. Stretching helps with posture, blood flow, and confidence.

3. Stretch your soul however you choose (Prayer, meditation, or yoga). Take a moment to spiritually connect your soul with a higher power.

Journal:

Intermission

I know you probably thought you couldn't commit for 30 days, but you are well on your way, and you are doing great! Whether you stuck with it and it's been 7 consecutive days, or it's been the 2 days on 2 days off, you are here now. Even if you stopped or skipped a day, the point is you came back, so let's get going.

My little sister
I was once in your shoes.
Enjoy these years you have nothing to lose.
Go here, go there, cut, color, and let down your hair.
Play the game but respect the field.
As long as you keep it real and express how you feel,
over time all broken hearts will heal.
Do your thang, don't let fear get in the way.
This is your time; this is your day.
Listen to your gut; it will show you the way.
Friends come and go, and love—well, love is not guilt, shame, or pain.
When he's the right one, he won't want to do you wrong, but if he's wrong, he will keep singing the same old song.
He's not the one and that's okay—love my dear won't stay away!

Love you first and love will last.

You are the key to our future; play it smart, do your part.
A wise woman knows you can't do it alone and can't be twenty forever.
Thirty is great, forty is better, fifty is freeing, and sixty and above sensational.
I've followed the footsteps and instructions of queens who came before me.
I've been in your shoes; you have not been in mine.
Always remember the torch comes and goes.
Knowledge is power. Wisdom comes with age.
Maturity comes from experience.
The more you experience, the more you grow.
Create your own path, be who you are, give back and shine like a star.

My Little Sister You Are . . .

Day 8

Start Living to Your Full Potential

"When you pass through the waters, I will be with you; and when you pass through the rivers, they will not sweep over you. When you walk through the fire, you will not be burned; the flames will not set you ablaze" (Isaiah 43:2, NIV).

Start believing that you are ready for the next step. You are ready to give your ideas and dreams a chance to blossom. Brainstorm, do your research, work hard, then take the next step. Life is passing you by. You can't be what you can't see. You have to visualize yourself doing what you want to do. See yourself doing what comes next.

Journal:

What is your next step in your career, business, education, relationship, or faith?

_____
_____
_____

30 Days to a Better You

What does that look like?

Day 9

Create a Routine and Track Your Progress

"You don't have to be great to start, but you have to start to be great."

–Zig Ziglar

Start scheduling time to work on your goals. Making a routine will bring you one step closer to achieving your goals; it will build your efforts and confidence. Keep a journal, use an app, or get a desk calendar and track your progress. It will help you stay motivated and keep you accountable for sticking to your routine. Creating a routine will help you:

- Prioritize your tasks
- Create structure in your life
- Be more efficient
- Help you achieve and track goals

Journal:

Day 10

Think Positively

"What you're thinking is what you're becoming."
—Muhammad Ali

Did you know that according to psychology our minds control our bodies? Positive thinking is not just a fluffy term, but positive thinking will help build your skills, boost your health, and can improve how you respond to unwelcome situations. Thinking positively is something everyone can do; it's a learned skill. Positive thinking will help keep you encouraged and ready to deal with the pitfalls life throws at you.

I personally listen to positive messages on a daily basis. Listening to positive messages daily has pushed me to take actions like writing this book! It hasn't been easy and requires daily attention, affirmations, and actions. I started by listening to inspirational messages first thing in the morning. I listen to various podcasts, read self-help books (like this one), and listen to inspirational music and speakers on a regular basis. Positive thinking helps me cope with the daily hustle and bustle called life. It also helps me see opportunities, wins, and lessons during moments of truth, frustration, and chaos.

How to get started:

- Smile and laugh more.
- Let go of your ego.
- Surround yourself with positive people.
- Train or retrain yourself to focus on positive thoughts.

"There is no royal, flower-strewn path to success. And if there is, I have not found it. For if I have accomplished anything in life, it is because I have been willing to work hard."

—**Madam C.J. Walker**, America's first female entrepreneur millionaire

Journal:

Day 11

Hold Yourself Accountable

"Accountability breeds response-ability."

—Stephen R. Covey

Start taking full accountability for your own life. Accountability is accepting who you are, who you will become, the choices you make, and the consequences that result from those choices. Being accountable for your life will empower you, foster success, and build your self-esteem. The good thing is that once you realize something doesn't line up with your beliefs you can change it.

Journal:

_____

_____

_____

_____

_____

_____

_____

30 Days to a Better You

Day 12

Start Looking for the Silver Lining

"In every difficult situation is potential value. Believe this, then begin looking for it."

—Norman Vincent Peale

Start looking for the silver lining in difficult situations. When you step back and take a good look at the situation, the silver lining always shows itself. It usually does not happen overnight, but it happens. It's a gradual process. With practice, you can challenge yourself to see at least one different way or outcome to deal with difficult situations.

Research suggests looking for the silver lining can help your overall well-being. It allows those negative feelings or thoughts to exist while pushing past the negativity to a more structured or controlled response. Having negative thoughts, emotions, or feelings is human. It's not all bad; sometimes negative emotions are the biggest reason why something or certain situations don't happen again. Because when something negative happened, you learned a lesson, took control, or learned to adapt to prevent that feeling from coming back. We can't control the world, but we can control how we respond, take control of situations, and find our own silver lining.

Journal:

_____

_____

_____

_____

_____

Shirley Walker-King

Day 13
Start Enjoying the Things You Already Have

"Be thankful for what you have; you'll end up having more. If you concentrate on what you don't have, you will never, ever have enough."
—Oprah Winfrey

Your happiness does not start once you reach your goals; your happiness is in your hands every day. Enjoy what you already have whether that is a job, car, house, clothes, family, friends, or eyesight. Take a moment to enjoy what you already have and be grateful. We sometimes take the simplest things for granted. When you enjoy what you have, you appreciate what comes next. Let's start by making your bed. Why? Because some people don't have a bed to sleep in. Think about it . . . you are fortunate to be alive – so enjoy life and what comes with it.

Journal:

_____
_____
_____

Shirley Walker-King

Day 14

Open Your Heart

"You can't break a guarded heart and a guarded heart can't be protected."

–Tracey Walker Pollard

Start being more open about how you feel. When you open your heart, you're giving yourself a chance to be happy which makes others around you happy. Try to enjoy a conversation with a new friend, have a cup of coffee with your crush, or just spend some quality time with your family. Little by little you'll see how your life starts to get brighter and how things start getting better.

We've all been hurt by someone we once loved, trusted, or even respected. It's called life and being human. You can't live your life with a guarded heart. It's time to move past the bitterness to better. Acknowledge the hurt, disappointment, and misused trust. Keep it in your head, so you recognize the signs, but don't let it control your heart.

Journal:

What broken thoughts do you need to let go of?

What broken emotions are keeping you from an open heart?

_____
_____
_____
_____
_____
_____
_____
_____
_____
_____
_____
_____
_____
_____
_____

"Every day, you have the power to choose our better history—by opening your hearts and minds, by speaking up for what you know is right."

—Michelle Obama

Day 15

Nurture Your Current Relationships

"Commit to the LORD whatever you do, and he will establish your plans."

—Proverbs 16:3, NIV

Start nurturing your most important relationships. Relationships are a very important part of life, and good relationships don't come easy, and they won't last without effort from all parties. Starting today, take time to build and nurture your most important relationships.

Take these steps to improve your relationships and watch your quality of life improve:

1. Make time for those who matter.

Good relationships take time and have to be developed. Dedicate 15 – 20 minutes of your day towards building and nurturing your relationships.

2. Communicate: be positive, honest, and open.

Good relationships start with being honest, open, and appreciative. Don't hold grudges and don't stop talking.

When something needs to be said, say it with an honest, open heart. Don't speak when someone else needs to be heard… just listen.

3. Don't jump to conclusions.

Relax and get all the information before reacting to harmful situations. Good relationships are usually transparent and are mutually beneficial.

4. Under promise and over deliver

Follow through, follow through, follow through. The best way to build and nurture relationships is to keep your commitment.

Journal:

_____
_____
_____
_____
_____
_____
_____
_____

Shirley Walker-King

Day 16

Stop a Bad Habit

"If your habits don't line up with your dream, then you need to either change your habits or change your dream."

—John Maxwell

Stop a bad habit and replace it with a new *good* one. Gossiping, smoking, and even judging others are bad habits. If you can't stop right away, start small until you can really let it go. Stop biting your nails or stop rolling your eyes when you don't agree with someone. On a deeper level, try to figure out what triggers such bad habits and address that. In order to do that, you must identify (be aware of) the bad habit; name it, then redirect it.

For example: If you want to stop cracking your knuckles, be mindful of the things or situations that make you go there. Once you see yourself doing it, stop and redirect your hand to do something else like pop a rubber band or stretch your hands out instead. Then give yourself a That-A-Girl or That-A-Boy for defeating the bad habit.

Pick one bad habit to stop today.

Journal:

What bad habit do you need to let go: smoking, cursing, stealing, drinking, or gambling?

Day 17

Concentrate on What You Can Control

"You don't have to control your thoughts; you just have to stop letting them control you."

—Dan Millman

Don't waste your time focusing on things that are completely out of your control.

Life is not easy, fair, or balanced. Spend your time on things you can control such as your A-E-D: Attitude, Efforts, and Determination. I know it's easier said than done, but you and only you control your attitude. If you are constantly upset, angry, and bitter, you will never be happy. When you have an optimistic outlook and positive attitude, things around you change for the better. Let's face it; happiness is not automatic. You have to put in the effort to be, find, and secure happiness, which takes dedication. Being happy and in control takes dedication and making difficult choices.

Journal:

Day 18

Forgiving Yourself

"No matter what has happened to you in the past or what is going on in your life right now, it has no power to keep you from having an amazingly good future if you will walk by faith in God. God loves you! He wants you to live with victory over sin so you can possess His promises for your life today!"

—Joyce Meyer

Forgiving yourself is a good thing; it frees you from bitterness and anger that holds you back from all the good you can achieve and experience. Negative self-talk is toxic, so don't let "I should have" cripple you. You are not perfect; everyone makes mistakes. Mistakes build character, and character is what people recognize more than mistakes.

"Then I acknowledged my sin to you and did not cover up my iniquity. I said, "I will confess my transgressions to the LORD." And you forgave the guilt of my sin.

—Psalm 32:5 NIV

Journal:

What do you need to forgive yourself for today?

BONUS: You should forgive others because staying angry at someone or something and holding a grudge can change an individual. It's very important to forgive others for their mistakes and shortcomings. Don't allow someone else's mistakes to guide your future.

"For if you forgive other people when they sin against you, your heavenly Father will also forgive you. But if you do not forgive others their sins, your Father will not forgive your sins."
—Matthew 6:14-15, NIV

Journal:

Release your anger towards…

I forgive _____

for _____

_____

_____

_____

_____

_____

Shirley Walker-King

Day 19

Cheer for Other People

"At the end of the day, it's not about what you have or even what you've accomplished. It's about what you've done with those accomplishments. It's about who you've lifted up, who you've made better. It's about what you've given back."

—Denzel Washington

Don't compare and despair. You really never know what someone else is going through, and you can't see the whole picture because you are not in it. Cheering someone up is all about taking the time to listen to them, empathizing with what they're going through, and helping them get a better perspective of the situation. Remember karma goes both ways! When you're helping others, you will often feel better about yourself, increasing the likelihood that your next experience will be a positive one rather than a negative one. So, start cheering for others; it will help you feel better, and it doesn't take away from your joy, happiness, or success. Believe me, there is way more than enough success, happiness, and joy to go around for all of us. You have yours. Now help someone find theirs.

Do you know someone who recently accomplished something? Won an award? Reached a new milestone? Take time to send them a card of congratulations. It's okay to celebrate others' success because you could be next in line with good news.

Journal:

30 Days to a Better You

Day 20

Be Yourself

"Find out who you are and be that person. That's what your soul was put on this Earth to be. Find that truth, live that truth and everything else will come."

—Ellen DeGeneres

Start being your true self. The true you is the person you are when nobody is watching. Learn to love and appreciate that person, flaws and all. Your flaws make you uniquely you. Who cares what others may think about you? You should be proud of yourself, honest with yourself, and learn to make you count. Focus on being in the present; become aware of your inner thoughts, strengths, and vulnerabilities. I know it's scary to be vulnerable, and that's okay. Remember you choose to whom, when, and how you want to open up to people. When you're comfortable in your skin, you can share yourself and your story with everyone or just a few people who you feel close to and trust. Always follow your intuition. The goal is to be true to YOU! Plus, as Oscar Wilde said, *"Be yourself; everyone else is already taken."* Now say this with me, "I am who I am, and I love being me."

Who am I—I am me
I am not yet where I want to be
But give me time, give me space
One day I will not be erased.
Who am I—I am me
I have hopes, and I have dreams
I have an insight and a vision that has not yet been seen
Who am I—I am me
I am a mother, father, sister, brother, and teacher
In God's eye I am a preacher
Who am I—I am me
I am a part of history that some refuse to see
A child of God on a journey to be free
Who am I—I am unapologetically me
Who am I is no longer the question because I am
working on who I want to be
A better me

Journal:

Day 21

Listen to Yourself

"The mind is everything. What you think you become."
—Buddha

What you believe to be true determines your beliefs and core values. As a child, we learn right from wrong, good and bad, and we unconsciously take on our parents' beliefs. Good or bad, it's the foundation of who we are. The good news is that the foundation can be re-laid. If you were not taught to listen to your inner voice, it's time to cut through the clutter to get to your inner angel, that voice that will protect you, lead you, and keep you encouraged. It's time to follow your heart and your intuition.

- Be mindful of everything you do, say, and post. Doing so will keep you aware of what's going on inside of you daily.
- Remember no one else knows what will make you happy and what brings your life into balance, so listen to what you have to say.

How you talk to yourself will determine your next move. Tell yourself these things daily:

- I love me some me.
- I make a difference in this world, and I have a purpose to fulfill.
- Today is a new day to do something positive.
- I will inhale confidence and exhale doubt.
- I am strong, confident, and beautiful.
- I am capable of achieving great things.
- (your name here) _____ you got this.

Remember, your thoughts carry power or pain, so think positively when you say I am...

Journal:

_____
_____
_____
_____
_____

30 Days to a Better You

Day 22

Push Past Your Comfort Zone

"The ultimate measure of a man is not where he stands in moments of comfort and convenience, but where he stands at times of challenge and controversy."

—Dr. Martin Luther King Jr.

Get uncomfortable. In order to be the best version of yourself, YOU must push past your comfort zone. We all have something we fear, something that makes your stomach turn just thinking about it. Whether it's the fear of public speaking, heights, rock climbing, snacks, spiders, intimacy, loneliness, death, crowds, rollercoasters. or being near large bodies of water, we all have that something. In order for me to push past my comfort zone, I had to shake things up a little. I relearned how to swim. I took a trip that I had no input in planning, and I started putting myself in new environments. Now, it's your time to shake things up. Remember growth doesn't come with comfort; growth comes in times of challenge, change, and adventure. Doing something new, different, and out of your comfort zone will make you a better person and give you stories to tell people you meet.

"You cannot do a kindness too soon for you never know how soon it will be too late."

—Ralph Waldo Emerson

Journal:

_____

_____

_____

_____

_____

_____

_____

_____

_____

_____

_____

Shirley Walker-King

Day 23

Say Thank You

"We must find time to stop and thank the people who make a difference in our lives."

—John F. Kennedy

These little magic words can make a world of difference. Take a moment to tell someone thank you. Saying thank you is one of the most important things we can do to show appreciation. As a child, your parents enforced the values of saying thank you to family and friends, so you should continue doing that because it makes people smile. Telling those you love that you love them adds value to your relationship and well-being. Telling and showing the people you love how much you appreciate them makes everyone happy and creates positive vibes that start a ripple effect and makes the world a better place.

Saying thank you:
- Makes you feel good and is good for the heart.
- Keeps you humble and appreciative.
- Shows compassion, kindness, and respect.

You can also tell someone:

- Thank you for being patient with me.
- Thank you for your loyalty and for being on my team.
- Thank you for pushing me to try harder at _____ _____.
- Thank you for lifting me up when I was down and out.

Who can you tell thank you today?

List 3 names: _____

_____

_____

Give them a call, send a text, or send an email to simply say thank you!

Journal:

_____

_____

_____

_____

30 Days to a Better You

Day 24

Spend Time in Nature

"For in the true nature of things, if we rightly consider, every green tree is far more glorious than if it were made of gold and silver."

—Martin Luther

Have you ever noticed when you go outside for a walk you seem to think more clearly? There is a reason why God made nature. Nature is relaxing. Fresh air, sunshine, and even rain helps melt away problems. Take time to take a walk, read a book in the park, eat lunch outside, go fishing, plant seeds, meditate, or work out. Spending time with nature in the sun's UV rays helps the body produce vitamin D, which is essential for good health. Be sure to wear sunscreen. ☺

Where did you go?

_____

_____

_____

_____

What did you do?

_____

_____

_____

_____

How did this time in nature make you feel?

_____

_____

_____

_____

Journal:

"Do not come any closer," God said. "Take off your sandals, for the place where you are standing is holy ground."

—Exodus 3:5, NIV

Day 25

Volunteer to Help the Less Fortunate

"Service to others is the rent you pay for your room here on earth."

—Muhammad Ali

Your life isn't so bad. If you have a roof over your head, food to eat, clothes on your back, and are able to live above ground and not six feet under, then life isn't that bad, and you have the opportunity to help someone less fortunate. There are so many people in the world who don't have a fourth of the items you have in your worldly possession. So, I encourage you to seek out these individuals and do God's work. Help someone who truly needs help. Step outside of your world, your comfort zone, and see how good you and I have it. Learn to be unselfish with your time and giving. Share your knowledge and expertise with someone in need of your help, guidance, hug, smile, or words of encouragement. Here are five ways you can volunteer:

1. Tutor, mentor, or sponsor a child. Call your local school, church, or youth program to find out when and how you can get involved.

2. Serve or connect with the elderly. Elderly people are the backbone of the community, but unfortunately, they are the most overlooked. Contact a nursing home or an assisted living facility to see if they could use a little of your time or expertise. Maybe you can teach a class, provide a free service, play bingo or checkers, or just read to someone who doesn't get any visitors.

3. Serve on a community board or join a community group. Most charities and non-profits need professional and administrative experience and knowledge. Due to funding, they may lack resources that you have readily available. Share your talent, knowledge, and resources such as accounting skills, graphic design abilities, website design capabilities, coaching/mentoring, and leadership skills.

4. Volunteer at a hospital or veterans' clinic. Hospitals and veterans' facilities have a wide range of volunteer needs that are suitable for people of all ages. Opportunities could include everything from manning the information booth to sitting

with patients, reading to children, face painting, food service, and offering comforting words to families and visitors.

5. Be a good neighbor. We have lost the interaction we once had with our neighbors. Participate in your neighborhood association's events, join the neighborhood watch team, assist with neighborhood beautification and park projects, or take it a step further and get involved with your local government agency. Knowing your neighbors and your local officials increases a sense of personal connection and responsibility.

Journal:

List ways you can volunteer here and do it:

_____
_____
_____
_____
_____
_____
_____

30 Days to a Better You

Day 26

Write a Gratitude Journal

"Gratitude unlocks the fullness of life. It turns what we have into enough, and more. It turns denial to acceptance, chaos to order, confusion to clarity . . . Gratitude makes sense of our past, brings peace for today, and creates a vision for tomorrow."

—Melody Beattie

A gratitude journal is a list of things you are grateful for today. Challenge yourself! Aim for one handwritten page of gratitude. This practice brings the positive into focus and moves the negative out of the frame. When you find you are stuck in a negative mindset, reach for your gratitude journal to set yourself back on track. You cannot always control what happens to you in life, but you can control how you perceive and learn from it. This is a good time to reflect on how far you have come and be grateful for what you have accomplished. Being grateful improves your chances of becoming happier and more content in your life. By being thankful for what you have, you will achieve true happiness.

Tips:

1. A gratitude journal can be physical or digital (Pick which one works best for you).

2. Remember to KISS "Keep It Short & Simple" (Don't overthink it).

    a. Date it, then write something like: Today I am grateful for… / Something I am grateful for is… / Another thing I am grateful for is…

3. Stay consistent; try to journal around the same time every day and even in the same place when possible. But if you can't commit to a daily journaling, don't feel bad or obligated. Just remember to do it when you can, when it feels right or when you want to give the universe acknowledgment or share goals or accomplishments.

Journal:

_____
_____
_____
_____
_____
_____

Day 27

Living Each Day with Purpose

"We must have a theme, a goal, a purpose in our lives. If you don't know where you are aiming, you don't have a goal."

—Mary Kay Ash

This will help you to remain present and focused. What can you do today to be more purposeful? What do you want to achieve? Whatever it is you want to achieve, you can do it. You have the power to achieve it; do your best and be able to live with the success of living life on purpose.

Steps to living your life on purpose:
- Make it a daily intention to look after your mind, body, and soul.
- Stop worrying about the "what ifs" of life.
- Set achievable daily goals and congratulate yourself on the small things.

- Remember that you only get to live each day once, so live it on purpose!
- Visualize how you want to live, love, and laugh, then be that person.

Journal:

30 Days to a Better You

Day 28

Let Go of the Anger

"Throughout life people will make you mad, disrespect you, and treat you bad. Let God deal with the things they do, cause hate in your heart will consume you too."

—Will Smith

Holding on to anger or resentment can provide serious emotional blockage that can appear in other areas of your life. To truly become a better person, ask yourself who you need to forgive in order to focus on what matters most - you. In order to move forward, you have to find the root of your anger. What caused it? Was it caused by fear, sadness, rejection, or guilt? This is not going to be an easy process, and you may need the help of a trained professional, and that's okay. Ask your medical provider, guidance counselor, pastor, or wellness advisor for a referral. Help is always just around the corner, so turn the corner. Remember anger is not a permanent emotion; it's temporary, but you have to make the right decisions to free up space for joy in your heart!

This is a not an easy task. Letting go of anger, resentment, and frustration takes time. Don't feel obligated or get stuck on attempting to address this today. Take some time to reflect on your emotions and what makes you feel angry. Write it down then release it.

Journal:

_____
_____
_____
_____
_____
_____
_____
_____
_____
_____
_____
_____
_____

Shirley Walker-King

Day 29

Understand Your Strengths

"For this reason I remind you to fan into the flame the gift of God, which is in you through the laying on of my hands."

—2 Timothy 1:6, NIV

As a human resource professional, too often I see talented individuals get stuck in jobs where their talent, leadership skills, and abilities are not utilized to their fullest potential. People sometimes get stuck at average… average job, average house, average spouse, and average life. For some, that's okay, and that's good enough for them. If you're like me and you strive to be more, do more, get more, or help more, then you have to figure out your strengths and learn to leverage them.

We all have something to offer. We are all in the business of doing business. If you know you can offer more and your talent, skills, and abilities are not being appreciated, then it's your responsibility to find someone who understands and supports your growth and potential. Your strengths are what makes you unique, so take note of your strengths and value them. Your strengths are usually a combination of your natural talent and what you enjoy doing (what comes natural to you).

Start by asking yourself, "What am I really good at?"

What are your hard skills/soft skills? Hard skills are learned abilities that require training, practice, and education such as coding, accounting, or speaking a second language. Soft skills are less tangible and more on the human side like getting along with others, listening well, and even being able to engage in small talk with strangers.

Write down what you do and what you're good at including both your hard skills and soft skills.

Then focus on those things and breaking them down to figure out what comes naturally.

If you are not really sure, ask around. Ask for feedback from people you know, like, and trust about "what they think you are good at."

Your goal is to find clarity by asking one or two people you trust, respect, or admire what they believe your biggest strengths are, and if they can include an example of when you demonstrated that skill, that would be great. Sometimes when things come so natural to us, we don't even know we've helped someone or a situation. We just do it and move on without reward or acknowledgment.

For example, I am a natural problem solver. I am open-minded, proactive, and non-conforming. I am very persistent and meticulous with peeling the layers until I get to the heart of the problem. One of my strengths is being solution-driven.

If you are still lost in the journey of identifying your strengths, take personality or assessment tests or profiles. There are plenty of free personality/strength finder tests online. Taking one will help you gain a better understanding of your strengths, weaknesses, and talents. It will identify certain traits that can help you define or redefine your unique qualities that make you, you!

Journal:

What have you discovered about yourself?

_____

_____

_____

_____

Shirley Walker-King

How well did I preform this task?

_____
_____
_____
_____
_____

What are my values?

_____
_____
_____
_____
_____

What are my fears?

_____
_____
_____
_____
_____

Day 30

Connect with Something Higher Than You

"Just as a candle cannot burn without fire, men cannot live without a spiritual life."

—Buddha

None of us are exempt from problems; therefore, you must always remember to equip yourself with the armor of spiritual balance. Spirituality is different for everyone. For most, it is the awakening process by which we begin to explore our own being and connection to a higher power. For me, that process is prayer and meditation. Whatever that process is for you, try to create an atmosphere of just stepping back and taking a moment to acknowledge the universe and all its greatness.

What does that look like? It could be:
- Reading a book (the Bible)
- Meditating
- Going into your sacred place to pray
- Lighting some candles
- Burning sage
- Soaking in a hot bath

All of the above will make you feel better which will open up the conversation to the universe.

Journal:

_____

_____

_____

_____

Shirley Walker-King

Guess what? We did it; you did it! You completed the 30 Days to a Better You Guide to Peace, Liberation, and Self-Reflection. You stuck with it and got it done. You put in the work, and now it's time to reward yourself. I hope you find a way to celebrate being you in a special way that brings you JOY. Say this with me: "I can, I will, and I did get it done for me and on my time all with God by my side!" I am so very proud of you. You made it your intention to finish this book, and you did, so enjoy your peace. Remember, there is only one you, so why not be the best you you can be!

Life will throw you some curveballs, and you may not excel at everything, but as long as you give it your all, do your best, and learn from any mistakes, you are a WINNER.

Dream big, have fun, and write down your dreams and goals. Put pen to paper to visualize what you want to accomplish, who you want to be, and why. Find a mentor and always celebrate your strengths.

Thank you for taking this journey with me! I had you in mind throughout this entire process, from the draft to the edits to planning and dreaming of the finished product. I can, I will, I did get it done for me… and you!

Testimonies

"I had to learn to put myself first in order to get myself back. I was so lost and didn't know where I went. With the help of my professional therapist and Shirley's posts, I found the best version of me."

—Mrs. R. Smith

"I didn't know how to get my confidence back until I read Shirley's posts and followed her on social media. I followed her 30 days to a better you posts, and each day I felt more and more like the old me. Actually felt even better because now I had a guide to follow and the courage to see it through knowing I was not alone."

—April Planters

Book Shirley Walker-King

as your next keynote, breakout session, host, speaker, moderator, panelist or workshop facilitator.

Topics:
Being a Power Mom, Creating a Balanced Life, Career Development, Leadership Development, Motivation & Inspiration, Parenting 101, Relationships-Love-Marriage and more!

Author | Speaker | Producer | Relationship Coach & Change Agent
Providing Resources and Results
NANPBW Inc. 2019 Business Woman of the Year

Website:
www.ShirleyWalkerKing.com

Facebook, LinkedIn and Instagram:
Shirley Walker-King

Twitter:
@Mrs.SWK1

About the Author

Former semi-pro basketball player Shirley Walker-King holds a Bachelor of Science from Amberton University in human relations and business. As a consultant, mentor, and coach, she calls on her experience as a military spouse to help others cut out the nonsense and "get down to business." Her diverse background empowers her as a change agent who helps women navigate their personal and professional journeys with vision, strategy, and action.

Shirley is a bestselling coauthor of Soul-to Soul and Power Moms. She was voted the 2019 Businesswoman of the Year by the National Association of Negro Business and Professional Women's Clubs, Inc. Shirley is also the winner of the 2019 Who's Who in Garland Neighborhood and the winner of 2020 Neighborhoods, USA Who's Who in America's Neighborhoods Award.

She is married to and hosts a podcast, "The King & I Relationship Podcast," with her husband, Vincent. They have one daughter, Valencia. In her spare time, she enjoys mentoring youth and young adults. Reading, dancing, and writing poetry are also some of her hobbies when she makes the time.

Learn more at www.ShirleyWalkerKing.com

Facebook | Instagram | Youtube | LinkedIn:
Shirley Walker-King

Twitter: MrsSWK1

CREATING DISTINCTIVE BOOKS WITH INTENTIONAL RESULTS

We're a collaborative group of creative masterminds with a mission to produce high-quality books to position you for monumental success in the marketplace.

Our professional team of writers, editors, designers, and marketing strategists work closely together to ensure that every detail of your book is a clear representation of the message in your writing.

Want to know more?
Write to us at info@publishyourgift.com
or call (888) 949-6228

Discover great books, exclusive offers, and more at
www.PublishYourGift.com

Connect with us on social media

@publishyourgift

www.ingramcontent.com/pod-product-compliance
Lightning Source LLC
Chambersburg PA
CBHW071003080526
44587CB00015B/2323